It's Never Too Late...

171 Simple Acts to Change Your Life

Patrick Lindsay

MJF BOOKS
NEW YORK

Published by MJF Books
Fine Communications
322 Eighth Avenue
New York, NY 10001

It's Never Too Late...

LC Control Number 2005937449
ISBN-13: 978-1-56731-755-8
ISBN-10: 1-56731-755-3

Originally published by Hardie Grant Books. This special edition published by MJF Books by arrangement with Lime Tree Productions.

Manufactured in the United States of America.

VB 10 9 8 7 6 5 4 3

It's never too late...

to make plans

Looking ahead takes you out of the daily grind.
Planning ahead brings hope.
Small plans first, with realistic goals.
Build confidence.
Then make bigger plans with bigger goals.
Always have plans.

"You are young at any age if you're planning for tomorrow."
Anonymous

It's never too late...

to say sorry

It takes courage
but it's worth the effort.
It releases you.
It enriches the other person.
It ennobles you.
It gives you both a new beginning.

"To see what is right and not to do it is want of courage."
Confucius

It's never too late...

to have a happy childhood

Draw a line.
Accept the past as a lesson for the future.
Praise yourself for surviving.
Use that strength.
Look ahead and smile with anticipation.

"You can't change the past but you can change the way you view it."

Anonymous

It's never too late...

to get a life

Slow down.
Look around.
Feel your heart.
Find the people and things that you love.
Care for them.

"There are many things in life that will catch your eye.
But only a few will catch your heart. Pursue those."
Anonymous

It's never too late...

to start again

Look at nature.
Nothing stays the same.
Why should you?
Use change wisely.
Like a sporting champion, change a losing game.
Keep the things that matter.
Lose the things that don't.
Set some goals.
Start afresh.

"Imagination is more important than knowledge."
Albert Einstein

It's never too late...

to lose weight

Decide to act.
Set personal small, medium and large targets.
Give yourself time, don't rush.
The key is patience.
Look at the positive results, however gradual.
Praise yourself when you succeed.
Forgive yourself when you slip,
look at the big picture.
Persevere.

"An ounce of prevention is worth a pound of cure."

Proverb

It's never too late...

to get fit

Think of yourself as a 'street' athlete.
Start slowly ... but start.
Set your own, personal goals. Be realistic.
Think how long it's taken to get unfit.
Walk one block, jog one block.
Swim half a lap, paddle half a lap.
Keep increases gradual, and manageable.
Be proud as you progress.
Never be afraid to ask for help.

"Success isn't the opposite of failure. A runner may come in last but, if he beats his record, he succeeds."

Anonymous

to fall in love

Open your heart.
(It's not easy but it's essential.)
How will love enter if your heart is closed.
Look ahead for love, not behind.
Love is waiting.
Don't chase it.
Be yourself.
Be open to possibilities.
Love will find you.

"In the end all we have is love and memories."

Anonymous

It's never too late...

to learn to paint

Allow yourself the chance.
Don't judge or compare.
Open your mind to the possibilities of your creativity.
See how children paint with abandon.
Look at the world around you with innocence.
See the colours.
Make a start.
Take a course.

"Every artist was first an amateur."

Anonymous

It's never too late...

to play golf

It's a challenge of the mind and body.
It's like life ... it's not fair ...
and you never completely master it.
But that's the lure ...
each round is a new adventure,
a tantalising test of your skill and patience.
But don't expect too much too soon.
Very few golfers are naturals.
Take lessons or you'll just practise your mistakes.
One good shot will bring you back for the next try.
Once you're hooked, you can
play for the rest of your life.

"Golf is a good walk spoiled."

Mark Twain

It's never too late...

to make a friend

Your mother was right ...
if you can count your true friends on one hand,
you're a lucky person.
Some of our best memories come from our friends.
The real joy of friendship is when you give.
To make a friend, give them your friendship.
They will reciprocate.
Treasure your friends.

"A friend is a person with whom I may be sincere. Before him I may think aloud."

Ralph Waldo Emerson

It's never too late...

to write a poem

We all have poetry inside us.
It's writing from our heart.
Poems can heal our hurts.
They can transmit our love.
Or our sorrow.
They are a beautiful gift.
Find some solitude.
Listen to your heart
and write down your feelings.
Let the words flow.
You'll be surprised.

"A poem weighs more than a novel."

Anonymous

It's never too late...

to find a soulmate

To have a soulmate you must be one.
It's usually a natural selection.
Soulmates find each other.
But you must be receptive.
It's a beautiful, rewarding friendship.
It has a strong spiritual element.
It can't be manufactured or forced.
To find yours you must look outwards, not inwards.

"A single soul dwelling in two bodies."

Aristotle

It's never too late...

to start a new career

Your career is not you.
It's not your life –
it's your job.
You can always expand your horizons
or change direction.
Remain positive.
Find a new work challenge –
one that inspires you.
Explore it.
Chase it with passion.

"Live the life you've imagined."

Henry David Thoreau

It's never too late...

to run a marathon

It's much more than a race.
It's a magnificent personal challenge –
as much mental as physical.
Learn as you train.
Take it gradually, in bite-sized chunks.
Prepare your body and your mind carefully.
Trust yourself.
Commit yourself to finish.
Keep your promise.

"We're all athletes. Some are just better and faster than others."

Anonymous

It's never too late...

to listen to your heart

Our world is loud, fast and chaotic.
We need time to pause.
To look around us.
To hear our heart.
It knows things your mind can't understand.
Take time out.
Freeze frame your daily life.
Be open to your heart.
Listen to it.

"The heart has its reasons, which reason knows nothing of."
Blaise Pascal

It's never too late...

to take a trip

Change the scenery of your life.
You don't have to travel far.
It's an adventure.
A chance to refresh. To learn. To compare.
To meet new people.
To make new friends.
To view things anew.
To grow.

"Travel broadens the mind."

Proverb

It's never too late...

to plant a tree

Think of it as putting something back into the earth.
Most of the time we take from it.
Help redress the balance.
Plant a new life. Nurture it.
Take pleasure in watching it grow.
After you plant one, you'll want to plant more.
Nurture them.
Encourage others to do the same.

"Nature never did betray
The heart that loved her."

William Wordsworth

It's never too late...

to dance

It's a celebration of life.
Of freedom.
Of joy.
Express your feelings.
Dance for your partner.
Dance for yourself.
Release yourself.
Savour the moment.

"Fine dancing, I believe, like virtue, must be its own reward."
Jane Austen, Emma

It's never too late...

to forgive

Forgiving releases us.
Until we forgive, we're imprisoned.
It allows us to look ahead.
It empowers us.
It gives us positive energy.
It opens up the future.

"Good, to forgive;
Best, to forget."

Robert Browning

It's never too late...

to listen to the birds

They link us with nature.
Take the time to observe them.
They manage to survive in our world.
And they do it joyfully.
They provide a gentle soundtrack for our lives.
Listen to their songs..

"The song was wordless;
The singing will never be done."

Siegfried Sassoon

It's never too late...

to laugh at yourself

Life is too short to take it too seriously.
It's easy to laugh at others –
much harder to laugh at ourselves.
But it's more rewarding.
It lightens our lives.
It brightens others' lives.
It builds self-confidence and self-worth.
It endears us to others.

"Laughter is the best medicine."

Proverb

It's never too late...

to smile

So few muscles needed.
So little effort.
So many benefits.
Smiling brightens our faces
and lights up a room.
It can disarm
Charm.

"Give a smile and it will be repaid."

Anonymous

It's never too late...

to tell the truth

Lies are a burden.
They entangle us and weigh us down.
Truth always fights to break out.
It usually succeeds anyway.
It's not worth the struggle.
Telling the truth clears the air.
Lifts the burden.
Liberates.

"When in doubt, tell the truth."

Anonymous

It's never too late...

to look at the stars

They promise so much.
They show us perspective.
We look at them and dream.
And hope.
And wonder.
At their unlimited possibilities.

"Ye stars which are the poetry of heaven."

Lord Byron

It's never too late...

to work for yourself

We all have the potential.
We need the courage, the determination
and the knowledge to make the break.
Learn the business.
Explore the risks.
Write your plan.
Make your commitment.
Keep your nerve.

"It is better to wear out than to rust out."

Bishop Cumberland

It's never too late...

to help someone

It brings joy to both parties.
It makes you a better person
and gives the receiver hope
and faith.
It's usually reciprocated.
It gives life greater purpose.

"The good is the beautiful."

Plato

It's never too late...

to take a stand

Sometimes we need to draw the line
because we know it's right
and for our own self respect.
Your heart will tell you when the time is right.
When it does, listen.
Then fight hard.
You will respect yourself.
So will others.

"Justice is truth in action."

Benjamin Disraeli

It's never too late...

to let yourself be happy

Be sad when you must.
Grieve when you must.
But don't be sad just because others expect it of you.
Take charge of your own happiness.
We are all entitled to be happy.
Seek light instead of shadows.
Treasure your happiness.
Share it.

"We don't remember days or years, we remember moments."
Anonymous

It's never too late...

to change a losing game

We all get in a rut sometimes.
The first step is to recognise that.
Then refuse to accept it.
Vary your life.
Explore new things.
Set new standards.
Take a different approach.
If you think you can, you can.
Remain positive.

"The winner sees a green near every bunker."

Anonymous

It's never too late...

to watch a sunset

It's one of nature's greatest wonders.
No artist can truly capture its aura.
No film can reproduce its splendour.
Watch it alone
or with a loved one.
Drink it in.
Feel humble but feel alive.
Be inspired by its magnificence.

"Everything has its beauty but not everyone sees it."
Confucius

It's never too late...

to cuddle someone

Life without touch is hollow.
Cuddles transmit love.
They give warmth. And hope. And trust.
The feelings flow back and forth.
A cuddle can make someone's day.
It can even save a life.
Cuddle generously.
And often.

"Never underestimate the healing power of touch."
Anonymous

It's never too late...

to be patient

We live with constant change,
with daily demands for quick decisions
and automatic responses.
Slow down.
Give yourself time to consider,
to sort through complicated issues,
to wait for responses.
Patience calms our lives.
It offers options.

"Everything comes to him who waits."

Proverb

It's never too late...

to say I love you

It sounds so simple.
And it is.
Yet it means so much.
To your partner.
Your family.
Your friends.
It's a gift.
Give it freely.
But mean it.

"How do I love thee? Let me count the ways."
Elizabeth Barrett Browning

It's never too late...

to visit a church

It doesn't matter which one.
You don't have to be religious.
Enjoy the peace and tranquillity.
Shut out the world for a while.
Take the time to explore your spirituality.
Think of your loved ones, your life.
Meditate.
Pray.
You'll be surprised.

"I like the silent church before the service begins, better than any preaching."

Ralph Waldo Emerson, Essays

It's never too late...

to know yourself

We think we do.
We know things about ourselves nobody else does.
But are we honest enough?
It comes with wisdom
and accepting our imperfections.
The more we know about ourselves...
... the more freedom we have.

"The spirit is the true self."

Cicero

It's never too late...

to fly a kite

Embrace the freedom.
Find the child in you.
Ride the wind.
Abandon yourself to its rhythms.
Feel the wonderful lightness.
And the underlying power.

"Remember a kite flies against the wind."

Anonymous

It's never too late...

to walk the Kokoda Track

Whether literally or figuratively,
everyone must walk their own Kokoda Track.
It's a physical and mental challenge –
mostly mental.
It pushes you past your boundaries.
It shows they are illusions.
It makes you reassess the important things in your life.
It teaches you mental toughness.
And humility.
And compassion.
It builds your confidence.

"They can because they think they can."

Virgil

It's never too late...

to listen

Take time to pause.
Even when you have a point to make.
Or when you're angry or frustrated.
Listen to the person talking to you,
to the world around you,
to your heart,
to your loved ones.
Listen to their words
and their unsaid messages.

"Knowledge is power."

Proverb

It's never too late...

to write a love letter

It can be to your beloved, your child, a relative, a friend.
Tell them of your love –
your special love for them.
It will mean so much.
Show you care – in your own handwriting.
An autograph of affection.
A personal gift in a cyber world.
A lasting memento.

"Inspiration is the act of drawing up a chair to the desk."
Anonymous

It's never too late...

to have a pet

It makes you a gentler person,
more compassionate, more tactile.
It expands your life and widens your focus.
It brings rewards:
unconditional love.
time for reflection,
warmth.

"To his dog everyman is king."

Anonymous

It's never too late...

to relax

Take time to pause.
Forget the coffee and the smokes.
Don't eat lunch at your desk
Take a walk in the park.
Browse in a bookstore.
Chill in a library.
Go for a run, or swim.
Have a laugh with friends.
Break the endless cycle.

"A pleasing land of drowsyhead it was."

James Thomson

It's never too late...

to cheer for a team

Turn your attention outward.
Find a sport you love
and a team you admire, or pity.
Follow their fortunes.
Get on board.
Lend your support.
Give them your passion.
Savour the highs and lows.
Enjoy the ride.

"An individual can make a difference, a team can make a miracle."

Anonymous

It's never too late...

to break away from the herd

It can take cold courage.
It's your chance to follow your heart,
lift your head up,
choose your own course.
It can bring disdain and abuse.
But it will also bring esteem
and admiration.
But, above all, it brings self respect.
Stand on your own feet.
Be an individual.

"No-one can escape from his individuality."

Arthur Schopenhauer

It's never too late...

to learn to cook

Open untouched worlds,
new sensations and cultures.
Become an entertainer.
Learn and make special recipes for special friends.
Stimulate your creative juices.
Invent your own recipes.
Be a culinary explorer.

"Tell me what you eat and I will tell you what you are."
Anthelme Brillat-Savarin

It's never too late...

to face your fears

Until you do, you remain in chains.
Never underestimate your courage.
Be positive in your approach.
If necessary, take it in stages.
Often your fear is outdated,
or based on a misunderstanding or misapprehension.
Once you break the spell, you're free.
Look it straight in the eye.
Back yourself.

"The challenge is not to win but to conquer the fear.
It's not the other people you have to beat, it's yourself."

Anonymous

It's never too late...

to make a choice

Don't spend your life weighing things up.
Golfers call it paralysis by analysis.
Draw on your experience.
Trust your judgement.
Learn to read your gut reactions.
You'll make mistakes, don't fear them.
You'll get many more right than wrong.
Allow yourself to be wrong sometimes.
Learn from those mistakes.
Mistakes are often the best part of life.

"The die is cast."

Julius Caesar

It's never too late...

to stop the world

This is essential.
We need time to reflect.
To chill.
To consider calmly.
To widen our vision.
To look for meaning.
We can't do it when we're
rushing headlong through life.
Take time to pause.
Walk. Sit. Pray. Meditate.
Think deeply.
Then live.
With renewed direction and passion.

"Time is but the stream I go fishing in."

Henry David Thoreau

It's never too late...

to enjoy the rain

Listen as it beats down.
Watch the drops as they hit the trees and flowers.
Smell its purifying freshness.
Surrender to it.
Feel it on your face.
Your hands.
Watch the puddles form.
Smell the freshness.
Let it sooth your spirit.
Wonder at the beauty of nature's renewal.

"The sound of the rain is like the voices of tens of thousands of monks reading sutras."

Yukio Mishima

It's never too late...

to be yourself

We're all similar.
But not the same.
Each of us is unique.
The world wants to classify us.
Place us in groups.
It's easier that way –
for politicians, advertisers, TV programmers, etc –
but not for us.
Fight for your right
to be yourself.

"Whatever crushes individuality is despotism, by whatever name it may be called."

John Stuart Mill

It's never too late...

to mind your own business

Grant others the same privacy you want yourself.
Resist the temptation to pry.
Use your energy positively –
you'll be surprised how satisfying that is.
If they want you to know, they'll tell you themselves.
Often ignorance really is bliss –
especially when gossip is so often wrong anyway.
Give respect.
And you'll get it in return.

"At every word a reputation dies."

Alexander Pope, The Rape of the Lock

It's never too late...

to ask for help

When you really need help, ask for it.
Don't let false pride hold you back.
It honours the giver.
It establishes a bond.
Later you can reciprocate.
That's how great friendships are formed.
And maintained.

"Seize the day."

Horace

It's never too late...

to prove them wrong

Never give up on what you believe,
or know is right.
If others doubt you,
desert you,
or oppose you,
use that as motivation.
But keep it positive.
Earn their respect.
And keep your self respect.
By holding your nerve.
And fighting to the end.

"Virtue is not left to stand alone. He who practises it will have neighbours."

Confucius

It's never too late...

to stop worrying

Separate the worry from the problem.
Figure out what you **can** do ...
... then **do** it.
If you have no power to do anything about it ...
... worrying about it won't help.
Allow things to take their course.
Options will open up.
When you stop worrying, you think clearly.
Open your mind to possibilities.
You'll be surprised how often the problem dissipates.

"Nothing in the affairs of men is worthy of great anxiety."
Plato

It's never too late...

to be kind

Most of us rush through life
and miss many of its greatest rewards.
Take a gentler road,
where you have time to talk to people.
Learn about their lives,
and their loved ones.
It will broaden your life.
It will give you compassion.
Accept their kindnesses.
Be kind in return.

"Repay injury with justice and kindness with kindness."
Confucius

It's never too late...

to find your true talent

Some know it from childhood.
Some never find it.
But we all have special talents.
Take the time to explore yours.
It may be disguised.
It may be undeveloped.
But trust your instincts.
Give yourself the opportunity.
It will be there.

"Genius is merely a greater aptitude for patience."

Comte de Buffon

to be fair

We can kid ourselves.
We can justify our actions.
We can deny responsibility.
But in the quietness of our heart.
We know the truth.
Your inner voice will tell you.
Be fair.
It's all about karma.
If you're fair to others ...
... things will balance out in the end.

"Only the actions of the just
Smell sweet, and blossom in their dust."

James Shirley

It's never too late...

to learn from mistakes

Take a wider view.
Look at the patterns in your life.
If there are recurring problems
maybe there are recurring mistakes.
Mistakes don't always look the same.
Look carefully.
Find the pattern.
Change your behaviour.
Learn.

"Experience is the mother of wisdom."

Proverb

It's never too late...

to open your mind

We all have preconceptions.
From our upbringing.
Our experiences.
Our surroundings.
The media.
Break your mould.
Push your horizons.
Broaden your thinking.
Open your mind.

"The mind is the guide and ruler of men's lives."

Sallust

It's never too late...

to reinvent yourself

You are what you make of yourself.
Not what others want you to be.
If you don't like the direction in which you're heading ...
... change.
Set some goals:
short, medium, long-term goals.
Consider the new path you need to take.
Take that path.
Back your judgement.

"The spirit is the true self."

Cicero

It's never too late...

to persevere

Those who accomplish things
are not necessarily the most brilliant.
Nor the most gifted.
They are the ones who never give in.
Inspiration is just the start.
Perspiration is what brings things to fruition.
Whatever the obstacle.
Whatever the opposition.
However long it takes.
See it through.

"Patience and time do more than force and rage."
Jean de la Fontaine

It's never too late...

to accept change

The only constant in life is change.
In nature, in society, in relationships, at work,
things change.
And they change constantly.
See it as part of the larger picture,
as normal.
Don't fight it.
Adapt to it.

"They must often change who would be constant in happiness and wisdom."

Confucius

It's never too late...

to be silent

Silence can show your depth.
It can draw out the truth.
It can be eloquent.
It can disarm.
It can soothe.
It can cool passions.
Sometimes it takes more courage than to speak out.
Sometimes it's just smarter.

"It is better to remain silent and be thought a fool than to open your mouth and remove all doubt."

Abraham Lincoln

It's never too late...

to make the first move

Winners have plans.
Losers have excuses.
Take the initiative.
Set the guidelines.
If you wait for someone else to move ...
... you're playing by their rules.
Be bold.
The risks are higher.
But so are the rewards.

"Taking the first step, uttering a new word is what people fear most."

Fyodor Dostoevsky

It's never too late...

to make your own luck

Prepare as thoroughly as you can.
Check out all options.
Rehearse.
Anticipate possibilities.
Look from different points of view.
Think through to the next step.
Focus fully.
The hardest workers tend to be the luckiest.

"God helps those who help themselves."

Proverb

It’s never too late...

to cut your losses

All things have a natural end:
stories, relationships, lives, investments.
The trick is recognising the end.
And accepting it.
How sad are champions playing past their time,
a love gone sour,
or a life without purpose.

“Know when to hold ’em, know when to fold ’em.”
Anonymous

It's never too late...

to grow old disgracefully

You are as old as your mind,
not the calendar.
Make each day a new day.
Refuse to relive old days.
Make bold plans.
Set new personal bests.
Journey into the unknown with abandon.

"Age is a matter of mind over matter.
If you don't mind, it doesn't matter."

Anonymous

It's never too late...

to grow something

Plant something and watch it grow.
A tree.
A flower.
An idea.
Hope.
Love.
An investment.
Nurture it.
Watch it develop.
Enjoy it with pride.

"There is no ancient gentlemen but gardeners ... they hold up Adam's profession."

William Shakespeare

It's never too late...

to find out the facts

We spend a lot of time jumping
... to conclusions
... or in at the deep end.
Stop a lot of angst,
Check before you leap.
Ask the obvious questions.
Do your homework.
Don't assume.
Challenge the obvious.

"Assumption is the mother of all fxxx-ups."

Anonymous

It's never too late...

to smile at a child

It's up there with the most beautiful sights on earth.
The smile of a child.
All innocence.
Full of untapped promise.
And pure joy.
Take the time.
Reaffirm their trust in humanity.
Make your day.

"'Tis unto children most respect is due."

Juvenal

It's never too late...

to read the directions

It may be the last resort.
It may spoil the challenge.
It may insult your intelligence.
But, then again ...
it may solve the problem.

"Though a man be wise,
It is no shame for him to live and learn."

Sophocles

It's never too late...

to find your soul

We all have one.
Some of us try to hide it.
Or ignore it.
But it's there.
Waiting.
At the centre of our being.
Waiting.
For our permission.
To guide us.
Allow it.

"The soul that rises with us, our life's star."
William Wordsworth

It's never too late...

to praise someone

It can mean so much.
Particularly if it's unexpected.
And unsolicited.
It spreads goodwill.
It warms the giver.
It encourages the receiver.
It brings dividends.
It engenders loyalty.
It bonds.

"Praise is the best diet for us, after all."

Sydney Smith

It's never too late...

to listen to your kids

They know stuff.
They don't know a lot too.
But the things they know are different.
And fascinating.
You can learn much from your kids.
About them.
About you.
About life.
Remember how frustrating it was
when you were a kid,
and people wouldn't listen to you?

"It's all that the young can do for the old, to shock them and keep them up to date."

George Bernard Shaw

It's never too late...

to say what you mean

It's simpler.
It's more honest.
It avoids confusion.
People respect you when they know where you stand.
It may be tempting to beat about the bush,
hoping to avoid confrontation,
or to avoid causing offence.
But when you truly believe something.
Say it clearly.
Stand by it.

"The greatest homage we can pay to truth is to use it."
Ralph Waldo Emerson

It's never too late...

to compromise

Things are rarely black or white.
Most lie somewhere in the grey centre.
There are other views.
Or other ways of achieving consensus.
Think about what you hope to achieve.
The path to it may not be direct.
You may have to surrender ground to progress.
Keep your goal in mind.
Adapt your means to suit the circumstances.

"It doesn't matter whether it's a black cat or a white cat as long as it catches the mouse."

Deng Xiao Ping

It's never too late...

to be a self-starter

Think of the freedom.
The empowerment.
The possibilities.
Chart your own course.
Don't wait.
Don't react.
Decide your aims.
Act.

"No one knows what he can do until he tries."

Publilius Syrus

It's never too late...

to grow

Move forward.
Every day.
Take every chance to learn.
From mistakes.
From advice.
By observation.
Through experience.
Push through your comfort zone.
Explore new subjects.
Meet new people.

"Only so much do I know, as I have lived."

Ralph Waldo Emerson

It's never too late...

to start each day afresh

Every dawn brings unlimited possibilities,
challenges,
hope.
Don't be shackled by yesterday.
Look ahead –
with optimism.
Create your future afresh.

"You cannot step twice into the same river."

Heraclitus

It's never too late...

to let go

To travel through life with lightness,
we must unload the things which weigh us down,
and hold us back.
Lose the baggage.
Regrets.
Grudges.
Hatreds.
Jealousies.
Vendettas.
Turn them loose.
Soar ahead.

"All that is human must retrograde if it does not advance."
Edward Gibbon

It's never too late...

to find balance

It's a bit like class:
hard to define but you know it when you see it.
You'll know balance when you feel it.
Seek it in your work.
Your relationships.
Your family.
Your diet.
Your passions.
Enjoy the glow.

"Skill to do comes of doing".

Ralph Waldo Emerson

It's never too late...

to listen to your body

It will talk to you.
Give it a chance.
Learn the signs.
The feelings.
The messages.
Good and bad.
Respect your body.

"Every man is the builder of a temple called his body."
Henry Thoreau

It's never too late...

to save your money

Start with the little things.
Your small change.
Your shopping pattern.
Then do a budget.
See where it goes.
Decide what's essential.
Stop any wastage.
(You'll be surprised).
Look at alternatives.
Make your money work for you.
You work hard for it.

"You can be young without money but you can't be old without it."

Tenneseee Williams, Cat on a Hot Tin Roof

It's never too late...

to enjoy the music

We all have unique soundtracks to our lives.
So free your spirit.
Surrender to the rhythm.
Let your mind chill.
Let your heart rise.
Music is what you make of it.
It calms.
Or raises passions.
It transports.
It recalls memories.

"Music, the greatest good that mortals know,
And all of heaven we have below."

Joseph Addison

It's never too late...

to push your boundaries

We all have boundaries.
They are almost all illusions.
Drawn by fear.
Or self-protection.
Or laziness.
Test some:
push them slowly at first.
See how they bend and disintegrate.
Learn not to trust them.
Take pride in pushing through them.

"... the desire is boundless, and the act a slave to limit."
Shakespeare, Troilus & Cresida

It's never too late...

to watch the waves

Smell the sea air.
Feel the spray.
It's one of nature's most soothing forces.
The endless rhythm.
The expansive power.
The constant ebb and flow.
The variety of the swells
Let the motion calm you.
Meditate on the magnificence.

"The sea is as deepe in a calme as in a storme."

John Donne

to have the best years of your life

You're writing your own story.
You're in charge of the plot.
Make each chapter better than the last.
You're only limited by your imagination.
And your will.
You may not hit every target.
But you won't hit any if you don't shoot.

"It's never too late to be what you might have been."
George Eliot

to cry

Sometimes it catches you unawares,
tears welling up without warning.
No matter how long ago,
no matter how often,
if you have sadness and grief locked away
it will eat away at you.
Let it out.
Release it.

"We need never be ashamed of our tears."

Charles Dickens

It's never too late...

to write

Your stories are like no other.
Your experience.
Your view.
Your hopes, losses, triumphs.
Are unique.
Record them.
Invent them.
Write them.

"You can only write about what bites you."

Tom Stoppard

It's never too late...

to live in the present

Most problems are fears of the future.
Or worries from the past.
If you live in the present they don't exist.
In the present you're as alive as you can be.
Your decisions are spontaneous.
Your heart is open.
Your spirit is free.

"Life is short and time is swift."

Proverb

to change plans

John Lennon was right ...
Life is what happens while you're busy making other plans.
Plans are guidelines.
Not regulations.
If they don't fit the circumstances.
Change them.
The greatest skill isn't planning ahead.
It's being able to adapt to life's unexpected obstacles.
And still look ahead with a smile.

"Times change and we with them."

Ovid

It's never too late...

to be curious

Curiosity opens possibilities.
It keeps you fresh.
And young at heart.
It acknowledges mysteries.
And challenges them.
It's grounded in hope.
It validates our existence.
And fans the inner fire.
To be curious is to be optimistic.

"The most useful gift for a child at birth is curiosity."
Eleanor Roosevelt

It's never too late...

to forgive yourself

Sometimes we're our own harshest critics.
Even more judgemental than our enemies.
Failure to forgive anchors us,
prevents us from moving forward.
Acknowledge mistakes.
Learn from them.
Resolve not to repeat them.
Then unshackle yourself.

"He that forgives gains the victory"

Arab proverb

It's never too late...

to make a wish

Take a walk on the bright side.
Wishes cost nothing.
They're your little secret.
A journey into your heart,
which often clarifies your true feelings,
turns them into visualisations,
then often sees them become reality.

"The wish is the father to the thought."

William Shakespeare

It's never too late...

to know your worth

Nobody knows us like we do.
Allow others to assess your worth.
But only if you respect them and their ability.
Back your own judgement.
Take a dispassionate look at yourself.
Don't ignore the down sides.
But don't mark yourself too hard.
Don't underestimate yourself.
Or be cowed into discounting yourself.
Value yourself.
And others will do the same.

"A man is valued as he makes himself valuable."

proverb

It's never too late...

to be better than you are

Set your aims high.
Don't settle for just OK.
Like an athlete, aim for personal bests.
Just don't obsess about it.
Use them as inspirational guideposts.
That will keep you interested.
And interesting.
Life will be more vital.
Opportunities will open for you.

"Life's splendour forever lies in wait about each one of us in all its fullness."

Franz Kafka

It's never too late...

to back yourself

It sounds so simple.
But it requires great faith.
Against all the doubters, the detractors,
the risks of failure and the self doubt,
believe in yourself.
If you don't back yourself.
Don't expect others to.
If you have the confidence in yourself,
so will others.

"He can who believes he can."

proverb

It's never too late...

to be content

It's so easy to be seduced by expectations,
to spend our lives searching ...
for better, bigger, more.
When we often have just what we need.
Think about the positives.
Enjoy your family.
Your health, your wonderful friends.
Your blessings.
Allow yourself contentment.
And treat improvements as bonuses.

"Content is happiness."

Proverb

It's never too late...

to wake up

Give yourself a wake-up call.
Life is short.
Often we wander through it.
There are no guarantees.
No 'Take Two'.
Remind yourself how fortunate you are.
Resolve to make the most of your time here.
Help make a difference in others' lives.
It will make a big difference to yours.

"The aim of life is to live, and to live means to be aware, joyously, drunkenly, serenely, divinely aware."

Henry Miller

It's never too late...

to make new friends

They're out there.
Waiting to connect with you.
In the end we're left with our friends, our loved ones and memories.
Keep your heart open to new friendships.
Every new friend is a new adventure ...
... the start of more memories.

"Man's loneliness is but his fear of life."

Eugene O'Neill

It's never too late...

to defy time

They say time is relative.
It is.
It's relative to the way you treat it.
As an enemy it's a negative.
A deadly countdown.
As a friend it's all positive.
A chance for exploration.
For growth,
For love,
For enjoyment.
Drink of it greedily.

"He that has time, has life."

Proverb

It's never too late...

to make some quiet time

Our senses are dulled by our rush through life.
We need time out.
Time for reflection.
It may seem a waste.
Or like giving your competitors an advantage.
But it will repay itself many times over.
In increased energy and creativity.

"Time is a great healer."

Proverb

It's never too late...

to be a late developer

Set your own timetable.
Don't allow others to dictate your pace.
Benchmarks are for average people.
You're an individual.
You have your own individual rate of growth.
Take the pressure off.
Allow things to develop naturally.
It's not important when you get there.
What matters is that you get there.

"Slow but sure wins the race."

Proverb

It's never too late...

to change your routine

Routines can be efficient.
Even comfortable.
But they can also be limiting.
Even mind-numbing.
Take control of them.
Be adventurous.
Vary them.
Explore new ways to travel to work.
New places to eat.
New destinations to holiday.
Expand your horizons.

"A change is as good as a rest."

Sir Arthur Conan Doyle

to have fun

It's often something we forget.
We're never too sophisticated,
or too old,
to have some good old belly laughs.
Take the mickey.
Challenge stuffiness.
Don't be afraid to look the goose.
People love someone who can laugh at themselves.
Try it.
It's contagious.
And great for your health.

"Everything is funny as long as it's happening to someone else."

Will Rogers

It's never too late...

to do something you love

The smartest people work at something they love.
If you can't do that
at least make sure you spend time
doing things you love.
Time will fly.
You will feel a great sense of renewal.
Power will return to you.
Treat yourself to it.
The real you will emerge.

"The best careers advice to give to the young is ' Find out what you like doing best and get someone to pay you for doing it."

Katherine Whitehorn

It's never too late...

to simplify your life

Every day our lives seem more entangled.
Work often dominates
And swamps our lives.
Balance is hard to find.
Locate your real priorities.
Untangle them.
Keep only the essentials.
Give away, or lose, the others.
The simple things are the most valuable.

"An artist is a man who says a difficult thing in a simple way."

Charles Bukowski

It's never too late...

to read a good book

It's one of life's great simple pleasures.
Take a journey.
Relax.
Learn.
Go back in time.
Or forward.
Be inspired.
Or challenged.
Share.

"A book should be either a bandit or a rebel or a man in the crowd."

D. H. Lawrence

to see the good

Too often we look for the down side.
For faults.
For frailties.
For base motives.
Take a different view.
Look for the good in people.
Appeal to their better instincts.
Draw out their good characteristics.
Often it's self-fulfilling.
Many people want to do the right thing.
But are too afraid.
Give them the chance.

"A good heart conquers all."

Proverb

It's never too late...

to keep exploring

Life is a journey.
A wonderful odyssey.
But some people just wander around in circles.
Caught in a rut.
Break out.
Become an explorer.
Try new ways.
New things.
Explore new paths.
Take the mystery tour.

"One man's ceiling is another man's floor."

Paul Simon

to be strong

You don't have to be overbearing,
to be strong.
Be strong in your convictions,
your love,
your friendships.
Be strong like a foundation stone.
It will centre you.
And allow you to step off with confidence.

"The thread breaks where it is weakest."

Proverb

It's never too late...

to share the credit

The temptation is always to take credit.
Especially when you deserve it.
But sharing it can be even more satisfying.
It rewards.
It encourages.
It's an investment in the future.
And the reflected glory often brings a warmer glow.

"It is more blessed to give than to receive."

The Bible, Acts 20:35

It's never too late...

to look for opportunities

It sounds so obvious.
But often, through pressure,
or haste,
or boredom,
we get so fixated on our aim
we miss opportunities on the way.
Expand your vision.
Open your mind.
Look for your chance.

"A wise man will make more opportunities than he finds."
Francis Bacon

It's never too late...

to imagine

Our most powerful asset is our mind.
Its powers are virtually unlimited.
And often largely untapped.
With imagination we can create new worlds.
And improve old ones.
Live our wildest dreams.
And dream our wildest lives.
Imagination has neither rules nor boundaries.

"The imagination is man's power over nature."

Wallace Stevens

It's never too late...

to stop blaming others

It's the easy way out.
It brings us no credit.
It gives others power over us.
Ultimately we must take control of our own lives.
Make our own decisions.
Cop the blame.
When we do, it liberates us.
Take charge.

"Chart your own course."

Proverb

It's never too late...

to speak in public

At first it's daunting.
But take it in steps.
First, know your subject.
(This is the essential element.)
Then, order your thoughts.
Practise –
first alone, then before friends.
If you're interested in what you have to say,
chances are so will your audience.

"A bold heart is half the battle."

Proverb

It's never too late...

to greet the dawn

It's full of such beauty and joy.
And promise of new days to come.
It will charge your batteries.
Give you new perspectives.
And time to consider them.
Feel the glow.
The warmth.
Consider the possibilities.

"Each time dawn appears, the mystery is there in its entirety."
Rene Daumal

It's never too late...

to remember

Our memories are a treasure trove –
our living photo album.
All the pivotal moments are captured there.
Even some we've jammed into the dark recesses.
Take time to visit your memories.
Spool through them.
Enjoy them.
Be sobered by them.
Learn from them.
Then add to them.

"The richness of life lies in memories we have forgotten."
Cesare Pavese

It's never too late...

to study again

It doesn't have to be formal study.
It doesn't need any time limit.
Study life.
Study the things which fascinate you.
Learn new skills.
Update old ones.
Explore.

"Knowledge is the most democratic source of power."
Alvin Toffler

It's never too late...

to enjoy your success

Too often once we achieve a goal,
we take it for granted.
It's part of the journey.
It's important to give ourselves some credit.
Otherwise we lose our sense of purpose.
Enjoying the victories gives us strength to continue.
And sweet memories to inspire us.

"A (success) = X (work) + Y (play) + Z (keep your mouth shut)
Albert Einstein

It's never too late...

to fight for love

If you know deep in your heart,
that it's worth fighting for,
then fight.
Sometimes you're the only one
who knows what's right.
And even if you fail,
you'll have the satisfaction of
knowing you did your best.
You can't do more.

"Love is everything it's cracked up to be."

Erica Jong

It's never too late...

to stay young

It doesn't mean fighting time.
We must grow.
We can even age.
But we can stay young at heart and in mind.
Look with young eyes.
Love with a young heart.
Recapture the wonderment.
Appreciate your surroundings,
your loved ones,
your friendships.
Look forward with hope and optimism.

"Youth has no age."

Pablo Picasso

to take the lead

You'll know when the time is right.
The moment will present itself.
When you are the best equipped.
The most experienced.
Or the most capable.
You owe it to yourself to grasp the chance.
Trust your instincts.
Show the way.

"A leader is a man who can adapt principles to circumstances."

General George S. Patton

It's never too late...

to bounce back

What goes around, comes around.
Sometimes the down times seem endless.
But they're part of a cycle.
Be persistent.
That's the key.
Keep the faith.
It may take time.
But you'll bounce back.

"The struggle is my life. I will continue fighting for freedom until the end of my days."

Nelson Mandela

to be compassionate

No matter how successful.
No matter how well you're travelling.
Be open to those who are struggling.
It's amazing what even a small gesture can do
for their confidence
and your soul.

"When kindness has left people, even for a few moments, we become afraid of them as if their reason had left them."
Willa Cather

It's never too late...

to learn to breathe

It's the most basic of human functions.
Yet few of us do it properly.
Relax.
Feel your breathing.
Just being aware of it will calm you.
Draw in the air slowly.
Let it charge you with its energy.
Spend some time savouring the feeling.
Do some homework.
Learn from the experts.

"If anything is sacred, the human body is sacred."
Walt Whitman

It's never too late...

to ask for what you want

If you don't ask, you won't get.
It's usually true.
Don't assume others know what you want.
Or need.
Don't blame them if you don't communicate.
Be reasonable.
Be fair.
But be clear.

"Ask and it shall be given you."

The Bible, Matthew 7:7

It's never too late...

to make a difference

Throughout history
individuals have made a difference.
You can too.
Make the effort.
Just trying will bring you satisfaction
and honour
and, sometimes, gratitude.

"Do more than is required of you."

General George S. Patton

It's never too late...

to be free

Too often we make our own cages.
Of the mind.
Or the heart.
We have the key to unlock them.
We only need the will to use it.
Set your mind free.
Make your own decisions.
Unlock your heart,
love freely.
Unlock your mind,
Live freely.

"Your freedom and mine cannot be separated."

Nelson Mandela

It's never too late...

to eat less

Eating is mostly about habit.
And opportunity.
If you want to eat less.
Have a good reason to do it.
Then it will make sense.
Set some realistic targets.
And enticing rewards for reaching them.
Then trust yourself.
And go for it.

"One should eat to live, not live to eat."

Molière

to love your work

Sometimes it's inspiring.
Sometimes it's monotonous.
Usually it depends on our attitude.
Look for the positives.
Every job has its own nobility.
Give your work the respect it deserves.
And you'll gain respect in return.

"Work keeps away those three great evils: boredom, vice and poverty."

Voltaire

It's never too late...

to sing

It's a life force of its own –
in happiness,
or sorrow,
in hope,
or despair,
in prayer,
or passion.
Singing can ease the pain
and celebrate the delights.
It transcends language.
It touches the soul.

"To sing is to love and to affirm, to fly and soar, to coast into the hearts of the people who listen."

Joan Baez

to find peace

Nobody can prevent you from finding peace.
Unless you empower them.
If something is stopping you from reaching it,
act on it.
If it's outside your powers,
stop worrying about it.
Peace comes from within.
Search inside yourself.

"A peace above all earthly dignities,
A still and quiet conscience."

William Shakespeare

It's never too late...

to use your skills

We possess many skills.
Many more than we admit.
Even to ourselves.
We've taken much time and energy to acquire them.
Don't ignore them.
Don't waste them.
Take pride in them.
Use them when they're called for.

"Skill and confidence are an unconquered army."

Proverb

It's never too late...

to share wisdom

It's rewarding.
It brings benefits to both giver and receiver.
Pass on hard-won experience.
Especially where it can stop suffering or pain.
Hand on knowledge generously.
It will be repaid tenfold.

"If you have, give.
If you learn, teach."

Maya Angelou

It's never too late...

to live and let live

We all look at life through different eyes.
There's no correct way.
Only the best way for us.
Make your own choices.
Grant others the same right.

"Life loves the liver of it."

Maya Angelou

It's never too late...

to clean out a cupboard

It can be a wonderful adventure.
A great empowerment.
A journey into the past.
A chance to jettison baggage.
An opportunity to make new plans.
A fresh start.

"The past is a foreign country; they do things differently there."

L. P. Hartley

It's never too late...

to give blood

The symbolism is so powerful.
The gift of life.
It's within our power.
It affirms our humanity.
It offers hope.
Think of the potential good you can do.

"Where there's life, there's hope."

Terence (c190–159 BC)

It's never too late...

to love unconditionally

Love can be liberating.
Or it can be confining.
Long-lasting love must be without conditions.
It must allow room for growth.
For expression.
For freedom.
For mistakes.
For forgiveness.
Unconditional love has no limits.

"Love sought is good, but given unsought is better."
William Shakespeare

It's never too late...

to change your mind

Take a view.
Make a point.
Make a decision.
But always keep your mind open.
Stay flexible.
Consider the possibility that you're wrong.
That there's a better way.

"Like all weak men he laid exaggerated stress on not changing one's mind."

W. Somerset Maugham

It's never too late...

to turn off the TV

Let it know who's in charge.
It's there for fun.
To keep in touch.
For information.
But every so often, just turn it off.
Ignore it.
Find an alternative.
Go for a walk.
Listen to music.
Read.
Talk.

"Television – a medium. So called because it is neither rare nor well done."

Ernie Kovacs

It's never too late...

to make your own decisions

Take advice.
Seek information.
Draw on others' experience.
Confirm your views.
But make your own choices.
Set your own course.
Be responsible for your own life.

"No decision is difficult to make if you will get all of the facts."

General George S. Patton

It's never too late...

to marvel at a butterfly

Wonder at their stunning beauty.
Their brilliant colours.
And elegance.
Watch their random journeys.
The way they ride the wind.
Their steely fragility.
A reminder of nature's glorious variety.

"Nature does nothing in vain."

Aristotle

It's never too late...

to be enthusiastic

Our attitudes influence others.
Especially those who respect us.
Lack of enthusiasm can crush their spirit.
Maintain your enthusiasm for life.
For others' lives.
It will boost your energy levels.
And heighten your enjoyment.
It will energise your mind
and open it.

"Every cloud has a silver lining."

John Milton

It's never too late...

to count the stars

Away from the bright lights,
they shine clearest.
They remind us of our place in the universe.
They speak of hope.
Of optimism.
Of the great scheme of things.
Of the infinite potential of life.

"We are all in the gutter but some of us are looking at the stars."

Oscar Wilde

It's never too late...

to trust your intuition

Learn to recognise that gut feeling.
That gnawing certainty.
That inner belief.
When you know what is right.
Too often we're swayed by others' views.
Have confidence in your intuition.
It's built from experience
and observation.
Take advantage of it.

"True creativity often starts where language ends."
Arthur Koestler

to think big

Widen your horizons.
Look beyond your normal limits.
See things in a larger picture.
Consider the next step.
The flow-on effect.
Opportunities will become evident.
Motivations will become clear.
Perspective will emerge.

"One must live the way one thinks or end up thinking the way one has lived."

Paul Bourget

It's never too late...

to find old friends

They're like gems.
Links to our past.
Sea anchors in a storm.
They bring solidity.
A chance for reflection.
A link in our life chain.
A continuum.

"The best mirror is an old friend."

Proverb

It's never too late...

to smell the country air

It brings us closer to nature.
A reminder of a less complicated life.
Without the city's noise.
Or stress.
Or pollution.
Where people talk.
The skies are clear.
And stars shine.

"God made the country and man made the town."
William Cowper

It's never too late...

to hope

Hope is part of our life force.
Never surrender hope.
We know life comes in cycles.
And an upturn can be just around the corner.
Hope helps us struggle through the desperate times.
It guides us through the dark.

"Hope well and have well."

Proverb

to find the beauty

It's there in everything we see.
Sometimes it's shining out at us.
Sometimes it's hidden deep within.
Look for the core beauty:
in nature's balances;
in the human spirit;
beautiful friendships;
the beautiful mind;
the beautiful heart.

"Beauty is eloquent even when silent."

Proverb

It's never too late...

to be human

Too often we seek perfection.
And despair when we don't find it.
There is glory in all facets of humanity.
In our struggles.
Our achievements.
Our failures.
Our imperfections.
Perfection can be an aim.
But it's a not a pleasant state for a human.

"Every man is as God made him, and often even worse."
Miguel de Cervantes

It's never too late...

to make contact

Whether a long-lost friend,
or a new acquaintance.
Break through the barriers.
Touch the inner person.
Renew old connections.
Make new ones.
Find common ground.
Explore new interests.

"Each person's life is lived as a series of conversations."
Deborah Tannen

It's never too late...

to find your rhythm

You know it when you feel balanced.
When the segments of your life
are moving in harmony.
When your mind is sharp
your body feels light
and lithe.
And your spirit is strong.
Seek that harmony.

"All God's chillun got rhythm."

Gus Khan

It's never too late...

to learn a new language

Think of it as a key to new adventures.
A chance to look through different eyes.
To explore new lands,
and cultures,
and people.
A chance to expand your mind.
To challenge old ways.
To extend your boundaries.

"The liberation of language is rooted in the liberation of ourselves."

Mary Daly

It's never too late...

to look on the bright side

Make this your starting point.
Look to the lighter side.
Choose happy over sad.
Love over hate.
Good over bad.
Hope over despair.
Put the dark side behind you.
That way the shadows will fall behind you.

"To me life is simply an invitation to live."

Sean O'Casey

It's never too late...

to make your house your home

Stamp your personality on your home.
Invest some love in it.
Give it something of yourself.
Your colours.
Your pictures.
Your favourite objects.
In return, it will welcome you
and your friends.

"Home is where the heart is."

Proverb

It's never too late...

to update your skills

Never be afraid, or too lazy,
to stay on the pace.
Let your skills constantly grow.
Challenge them.
Build on them.
Share them.
And draw from others' skills.
Use your experience.
But keep it current.

"They know enough who know how to learn."

Henry Adams

It's never too late...

to say thank you

It takes so little.
Yet it means so much.
Make the effort.
No matter how late.
Mean it.
Say it generously.
It lifts spirits.
It maintains friendships.
And seals love.

"Who gives not thanks to men, gives not thanks to God."
Arab proverb

It's never too late...

to fail

We can't progress without failing.
Fear of failure holds us back.
Allow yourself to possibility of failing.
Most successful people fail far more often than they succeed.
But they persist.
Failing is just improving the odds
of succeeding next time.

"I would sooner fail than not be among the greatest."
John Keats

It's never too late...

to go forward

If you're marking time,
you're going backward
as the world moves past you.
Look ahead.
Aim high.
Push on.
Grow.

"If there is no struggle, there is no progress."
Frederick Douglass

It's never too late...

to be dignified

Live with style.
Win, lose or draw
with elegance.
Carry yourself lightly.
Give more than you take.
Praise more than you criticise.
Tread gently on the earth.

"Better wit than wealth."

Proverb

to love life

Consider the alternative.
Have the time of your life.
It's up to you.
You can live flat out.
Or you can slowly rust.
Be the best you can.

"Life is short and time is swift."

Proverb

It's never too late...

to find the edge

We set boundaries for safety.
From fear.
Because of habit.
Test them.
See why you drew them.
Push against them.
Break through them.
Feel the exhilaration.

"For what is freedom, but the unfettered use
Of all the powers which God for use had given."

Samuel Taylor Coleridge

It's never too late...

to keep your word

Your word is unbreakable.
Make it unshakeable.
Don't promise if you can't deliver.
Always deliver if you promise.

"A few honest men are better than numbers."

Oliver Cromwell

It's never too late...

to think

So often we don't.
We act, then think.
Take the time.
Avoid distractions.
Concentrate.
Wash problems through your mind.
Consider consequences.
Project ahead.
Do some homework.

"Thinking is seeing."

Honore de Balzac

It's never too late...

to do something great

Never underestimate your potential.
Or discount your ability.
Most great achievements are based on perseverance.
Believe in yourself.
Persist.
When others give in,
keep going.
When you falter,
have faith
and surge ahead.

"Be not afraid of greatness."

William Shakespeare

It's never too late...

to be on time

It's a compliment to others.
A chance to observe.
To eliminate pressure.
To calm down.
To organise.
To improve your chances of success.

"Punctuality is the politeness of kings."

Proverb

to mean no

If the decision is important,
mean it.
Consider it.
Discuss it.
Make it.
Stick to it.

"What part of no don't you understand?"

Anonymous

It's never too late...

to wonder

Look with innocence.
Drink with your eyes.
See the mystery in nature.
In people.
Ponder it.

"There are many wonderful things and nothing is more wonderful than man."

Sophocles

It's never too late...

to finish it

No matter how long.
No matter how hard.
Come back to it.
Look at it anew.
Seek help.
If it needs finishing,
do it.
Feel the release.
Move on.

"The end crowns the work."

Proverb

It's never too late...

to live for today

Only today is certain.
We're not guaranteed tomorrow.
Plan for tomorrow.
But live in the present.

"No time like the present."

Proverb